A New Penguin Leunig

Michael Leunig's words and pictures were first published in Australia in 1965. He was born in Melbourne and now lives on a farm in north-eastern Victoria.

A New Penguin Leunig comprises pieces that have previously appeared in the Melbourne *Age* and the *Sydney Morning Herald.*

Also by Michael Leunig

The Penguin Leunig
The Second Leunig
The Bedtime Leunig
A Bag of Roosters
Ramming the Shears
The Travelling Leunig
A Common Prayer
The Prayer Tree
Common Prayer Collection
Introspective
A Common Philosophy
Everyday Devils and Angels
A Bunch of Poesy
You and Me
Short Notes from the Long History of Happiness
Why Dogs Sniff Each Other's Tails
Goatperson
The Curly Pyjama Letters
The Stick
Poems: 1972–2002
Strange Creature
Wild Figments

Michael Leunig

A New Penguin Leunig

PENGUIN BOOKS

PENGUIN BOOKS

Published by the Penguin Group
Penguin Group (Australia)
250 Camberwell Road, Camberwell, Victoria 3124, Australia
(a division of Pearson Australia Group Pty Ltd)
Penguin Group (USA) Inc.
375 Hudson Street, New York, New York 10014, USA
Penguin Group (Canada)
90 Eglinton Avenue East, Suite 700, Toronto ON M4P 2Y3, Canada
(a division of Pearson Penguin Canada Inc.)
Penguin Books Ltd
80 Strand, London WC2R 0RL, England
Penguin Ireland
25 St Stephen's Green, Dublin 2, Ireland
(a division of Penguin Books Ltd)
Penguin Books India Pvt Ltd
11 Community Centre, Panchsheel Park, New Delhi – 110 017, India
Penguin Group (NZ)
Cnr Airborne and Rosedale Roads, Albany, Auckland, New Zealand
(a division of Pearson New Zealand Ltd)
Penguin Books (South Africa) (Pty) Ltd
24 Sturdee Avenue, Rosebank, Johannesburg 2196, South Africa

Penguin Books Ltd, Registered Offices: 80 Strand, London WC2R 0RL, England

First published by Penguin Group (Australia), a division of Pearson Australia Group Pty Ltd, 2005

10 9 8 7 6 5 4 3 2 1

Printed in Australia by BPA Print Group Pty Ltd

National Library of Australia
Cataloguing-in-Publication data:

Leunig, Michael, 1945– .
A new Penguin Leunig.
ISBN 0 14 300480 8.
1. Australian wit and humor, Pictorial. 2. Caricatures and cartoons
– Australia. I. Title.

741.5994

www.penguin.com.au

GLOSSARY OF CHARACTERS IN THIS BOOK

SULPHUR-CRESTED COCKATOO A successful, raucous and cheeky Australian bird with vandalistic tendencies occurring in large flocks

BODGIE (*boj*-ee) A stylish, rock'n'roll-inspired Australian male street hooligan of the 1950s era. His female companion was called a widgie (*wij*-ee)

OSAMA BIN LADEN A notorious and elusive figure

JOHN HOWARD An Australian prime minister, also a notorious and elusive figure but drearier than Osama

MR CURLY An elusive figure who is irrelevant and out of step with society, but quite contented

GEORGE A troubled American president

JESUS A radical interested in the phenomenon of hypocrisy who was executed for proposing that enemies are to be loved. Seriously out of step with society

ELVIS A legendary singer who was much admired by bodgies and widgies

IAN THORPE A fashionable and popular Olympic-champion swimmer

DAVID HICKS A popular young Australian scapegoat held without charge in Guantanamo Bay prison on suspicion of terrorist activities. Another person out of step with society

COLIN POWELL A soldier, an American secretary of state and a mystery

BASIL A worried wet leftie

STEVE ANVILBANGER A troubled, right-wing, warmongering newspaper columnist addicted to a deadly cocktail of whiskey, Prozac and Viagra. Also out of step with society

FOX TERRIER A successful, cheerful and spirited dog once favoured by the working class because of its courage, vim and playfulness. The fox terrier is medium in size, well tempered and sociable; it makes an excellent watchdog and rodent-killer, and there is no finer or more uplifting companion in all the world for a person who is out of sorts or out of step with society. Highly recommended

Dear Mr Curly.

I am writing to you from the South Pole where I have come to escape the heat of Summer. Or is it the North Pole? I'm not sure where I am. Does this mean I have bi-polar disorder? Regardless, I have discovered the joy of Penguins.

yours truly.

Vasco Pyjama

Leunig

...welcome to the first day of the rest of your life and to get started we'll make a list of all the silly things you did yesterday...
Leunig

George, darling ... come and see a beautiful thing: the couch potatoes are coming up!

Leunig

Nobody mentions any more
The weapons of mass destruction,
Except the cockatoo next door
Who got such good instruction.

He screams it to the morning sun
He screams it to the night
Reminding each and every one
Of why the war was right.

You can't re-educate a bird
By spin or sleaze or suction
He simply loves to have it heard,
"Weapons of mass destruction!"

Leunig

I've been such
a terrible mother...
he's all dreamy and
sensitive and
loving...

Don't be so
hard on yourself.
It could be a
birth defect.

Leunig

If this world should worsen,
A sulphur-crested person
Is what I want to be;
I'd fly into a tree
And do some squawking.
Now that normal talking
Cannot express
Feelings of such dreadfulness;
And all my failed beseeching
Would turn to screeching.

Leunig

It had been another sad and terrible week ...

... but the life coach (the grey shrike thrush) arrived on the doorstep.

WHAT NOW LIFE COACH ..? WHAT CAN BE DONE?

REALLY? DO YOU THINK SO? IS IT POSSIBLE?

YES! YES! OF COURSE ... YOU'RE ABSOLUTELY RIGHT!

It didn't take long.

THANKS LIFE COACH THANKYOU SO MUCH.

Leunig

Should we adopt a shoot-to-kill policy towards suspected evil-doers ?

...it's an interesting idea but it might be simpler just to vote them out of office...
Leunig

VOX POP

"SHOULD POLITICIANS BE TORTURED TO MAKE THEM TELL THE TRUTH"?

Dave (waiter) Manly NSW

"... I don't condone torture but I think the idea of interviewing them with electric wires attached to their private parts has some merit. Also, the concept of Howard, Downer and Ruddock in a nude human pyramid is fairly repugnant, but it could reveal some interesting information."

Fiona (psychologist) Carlton VIC

"... I'm all for it. It wouldn't make them tell the truth, nothing would, but it would be nice to torture them just for the pleasure of it. If I saw Howard, Downer and Ruddock in a nude human pyramid I'd take my hat pin and start jabbing it into all those bottoms ... I couldn't resist."

Wendy (designer) Sydney

"...What a fabulous concept. Yes, I like it. Definitely. I can just see it: Howard, Downer and Ruddock all naked and stacked on top of each other: a nude human pyramid. How wonderfully revolting. The trouble is that they'd probably love it."

Dave (waiter) Manly NSW

"... It's me again. I forgot to mention the bit about bestial acts. Well ... when we've got them on the nude pyramid, we should make them simulate bestial acts too. I just wanted to make that clear. That's all. Thank you."

Leunig

Mrs Pussington Bigge of Toorak prepares for Melbourne Cup day with her dressmaker, Raoul of Richmond.
Leunig

There was an old bodgie
called Wayne
Who smoked cigarettes down
a lane
With a look on his face
Of astonishing grace
And awful emotional pain.

THE NEWS

I made my morning cup of tea
And turned the wireless on;
The news I heard astounded me:
"Today the world is gone."

I drew the curtains open wide
And yes, the news was true;
Everything was gone outside
Except the sky of blue.

Osama was to blame, they said;
The evil dirty swine.
I yawned and waddled back to bed.
"And now the weather; fine!"

Leunig

WARMONGERS
OLD AND NEW WARS
• POLISHED
• REPACKAGED
• PROMOTED
WARS ARE US
That used to be a flower shop...
Leunig

Ah well ... I suppose we'd better look and see what New Year resolutions America has made for us ...
Leunig

I WISH you ALL a HORRIBLE summer, an awful Christmas and a terrible New Year.
Leunig

... and not only do you get the missiles, you get a lifetime supply of enemies, FREE, plus... we throw in this beautiful tee-shirt...

Leunig

THE THREE HAPPY AUSTRALIANS

PLANT YOURSELF IN THE GARDEN

You go into the garden. It's a good place to grow.

You pull out a little weed; and some nasty little worry leaves your mind. How fascinating!

And there! A tiny ant. So bright and brave. It could be you. Could it?

And look at that rose! You are reminded of your true love. So beautiful... and with sharp thorns.

Now contemplate the compost heap. It's just like your mind, your memory, your history. Breaking down but getting richer.

Ah-ha! The trellis. Full of beans and peas. <u>You</u> need a trellis sometimes. We all need a little support.

Oh dear. A stem has broken. Something has come to nothing. A hope is dashed.
But it's O.K. You will grow back. The sun will shine again.

But look at that beautiful, luxuriant fern. You are reminded of the book you want to write. Some sort of fabulous unfurling from an exotic part of your mind.

A bird sings and flits by. It scratches in the soil. Your heart is a bird. It flies up towards the sun.

The creeper needs cutting back. The petty worries, the nagging inhibitions, the nasty and the narrow. Those who drag you down. Cut yourself free.

Oh look at that! A new leaf! You can always turn over a new leaf. It will turn itself back again of course.

Ah yes, the garden, the fruits, the shoots, the blooms, the fragrance. The light and the shade. And you... you are in love and growing...

Leunig

PREVAILING WITH CONFIDENCE AND AUTHORITY. lesson 23: "STARING DOWN"
HOW TO STARE DOWN A PERSON WHO HAS JUST DECLARED AMERICA "A @★#! OF A NATION" AND PRESIDENT BUSH "A TOTAL ★!★@!#★!"
1.
2.
3.
4.
Leunig

BAN THE BUSINESS BURQA

Ban the suit:
The businessman's burqa.

Men trapped and submissive.
Men oppressed and hidden.
Men as property.

Fundamentalist garment.
Not in our country!
Zero tolerance.
Free men from the business burqa.
Garment of misery.

No more cultural baggage.
Protect our cherished values.
Protect our open society.
Say no to medieval ways.
Ban the business burqa!

Leunig

...happy New Year Rosie.
...happy new beer Bert.
SMOKERS
Leunig

Those underworld people are out of control ...
MURDER
HIT MAN

Yes, but they're sweethearts compared with those overworld people ...
Leunig

Leunig

ALSO PART OF THE EASTER STORY
Last chance, Jesus... Be a nice chap and convert to Christianity: pleasant, sensible, polite Christianity, and we might release you from detention...
NEVER!
Leunig

HOME NO HOME
HOMES THREE HOMES

CLICHÉ AGGRO TENNIS WINNER ICONS.
Take one or two daily during summer until everything becomes numb, meaningless and rather silly.
Leunig

Right-Wing Think Tank

Leunig

" A man's work is nothing but the long journey to recover the two or three great and simple images which first gained access to his heart " ALBERT CAMUS
Leunig

YOU
ARE
FREE
Leunig

WAR
WAR
Leunig

NEW MIRACLE FORCE DOES EVERYTHING
FORCE
Leunig

Mr Curly in your dinghy
What's that funny little thingie ?
What's that lovely, happy thingie ?
Little precious, lovely thingie ;
Such a lost and lonely thingie ;
Where's that funny little thingie ?
Mr Curly in your dinghy.

...watch out for Basil;
he's as mad as a human...
Leunig

groan therapy
groan 1 v. make deep sound expressing pain or grief or disapproval; be oppressed or loaded. 2 n. sound made in groaning.
THREE USEFUL POSITIONS
Leunig

CHRISTMAS DAY... A CELEBRATION OF FAMILY

COUSIN FIONA

MUM

GRANDPA
Leunig

YET ANOTHER PICTURE WITH THE WRONG CAPTION

Increasing numbers of children in Iraq do not have enough food to eat, and more than a quarter are chronically undernourished, a UN report says. Malnutrition rates in children under five have almost doubled since the US-led intervention – to nearly 8% by the end of last year, it says. UN specialist on hunger, Jean Ziegler, who prepared the report, blames the worsening situation in Iraq on the war led by coalition forces.

– News report

Leunig

Welcome, viewers across Australia. The Prime Minister has been chained and padlocked and placed in the steel box, which has been bolted shut and all joins welded.
The whole thing has been cased in reinforced, hardened concrete and is now being lowered into the icy waters of the lake, which is one hundred metres deep.
Can the Prime Minister get out of this one, ladies and gentlemen ... ? Let us see. Can he do it? CAN HE ESCAPE?
THERE HE IS! IT'S HIM! There he goes! That's him up there in the jet plane. He's flying away. He's doing an overseas trip. It's him! It's him! He's getting away...
AMAZING, ladies and gentlemen. AMAZING! He's done it.
He's done it again.
Leunig

IS THIS HOWARD'S FACE?

A former Canberra Parliament House tea lady who wishes to remain anonymous has come forward with what some experts believe could be proof of the Prime Minister's more human and compassionate nature. The woman has produced a piece of fabric, now dubbed "the Canberra tea-towel", which appears to bear the imprint of John Howard's weeping face.

"One afternoon he rushed into the tea room in a desperate state, grabbed a tea-towel, buried his face in it and wailed pitifully for about a minute," said the retired tea lady, who elaborated that the PM was repeatedly sobbing the phrase, "How could they do this?"

"When he finished he handed me the tea-towel and asked me to destroy it and not tell anyone what I'd seen. I took the tea-towel home, and next morning noticed the amazing marks on the fabric which showed the Prime Minister's face. It was like a miracle."

Experts at ANU have confirmed that the imprint "appears to be authentic but evidence of actual compassionate weeping has yet to be found".

Leunig

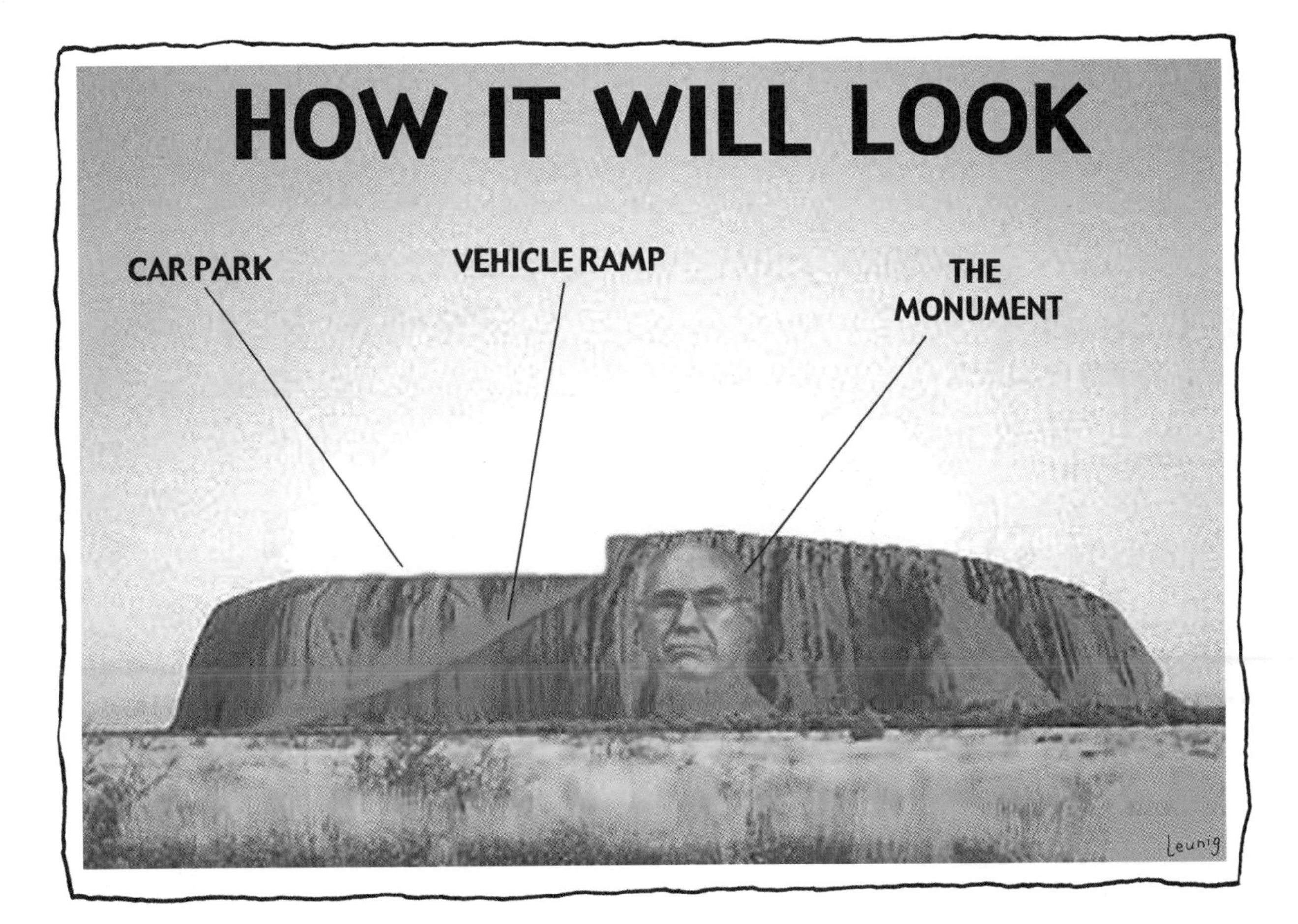
HOW IT WILL LOOK
CAR PARK
VEHICLE RAMP
THE
MONUMENT
Leunig

Leunig

Not only do the bastards grind you down
They also write the story of your life
And then they publish it across the town:
How you caused yourself a lot of strife.
How you'd lost your way and hadn't seen,
How you'd caused yourself a lot of hurt,
And what a crazy bastard you had been
To go and grind your life into the dirt.

Leunig

EXCUSE ME...
we're the three wise men and we're going to see the Prince of peace. Would you mind stepping aside please...
Leunig

A foreign Policy
A Surgical strike
Hollywood in a Nutshell
Hiroshima in a Nutshell
A Flower
Another flower
Leunig

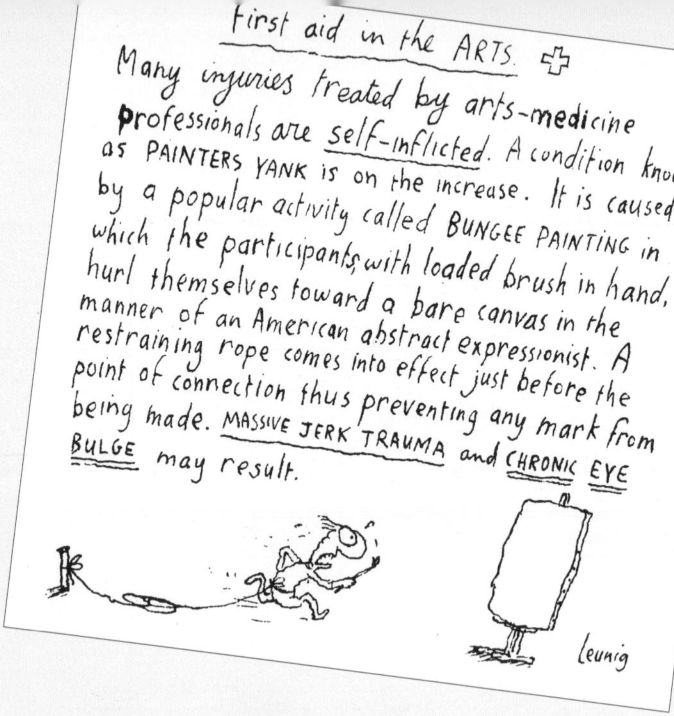

First aid in the ARTS ✚

Many injuries treated by arts-medicine professionals are self-inflicted. A condition known as PAINTERS YANK is on the increase. It is caused by a popular activity called BUNGEE PAINTING in which the participants, with loaded brush in hand, hurl themselves toward a bare canvas in the manner of an American abstract expressionist. A restraining rope comes into effect just before the point of connection thus preventing any mark from being made. MASSIVE JERK TRAUMA and CHRONIC EYE BULGE may result.

Leunig

FIRST AID in the ARTS ✚

Arts medicine is a HUGE INDUSTRY. Already there are an estimated 30,000 ARTS INJURY CLINICS in Australia treating such conditions as spontaneous combustion, "curators trousers" and bristle neck, an ailment whereby an art experience is SO electrifying that the hairs on the back of the neck stand on end and will not lie down again.

The pain is excruciating when I wear my cravat...

Hmm... we might have to put you on FUMÉ BLANC for a while...

NAKED MUM IN TRUCK CAFÉ SEX RAMPAGE

LORD IN NUDE FOX HUNT SHOCK

FIRST AID in the Arts ✚

Visual experience can sometimes be too big and it becomes STUCK in the eye of the beholder. Swift removal is necessary or else brain damage will occur. EYE-TO-EYE RESUSCITATION, properly given, will get the patient seeing again.

NOW SHOWING "THE PIANO"

CORRECT POSITION

Leunig

the definition of the word "artist" continues to broaden. For instance:–

"Bianca, you have revealed me to myself and at last I understand who I am and what I am capable of. So I say to you, in all earnestness and sincerity, stop calling yourself a fingernail technician and declare yourself —

AN ARTIST!"

Leunig

THE BEST THINGS IN LIFE (FREE)

WICKED THINGS (AT MARKED PRICES)

FIRST AID in the ARTS...

The mysteriously named affliction "CURATORS TROUSERS" is in fact a condition originating in the chin. Excessive contemplative stroking causes the erectile tissue in the chin to swell grotesquely. In chronic cases the engorgement may activate a CHAIN REACTION OF TUMESCENCE throughout the entire body and indeed throughout entire sections of the ARTS COMMUNITY with hideous consequences.

Leunig

60 LASHES

Leunig

THE Ken Done CONDOM

TODAY'S F.A.Q.s

Q. Why are so many children in crisis and cracking up?

A. BECAUSE WE'VE GOT SUCH A GREAT DEMOCRACY.

Q. Why are the children cracking up?

A. BECAUSE WE'RE THE LUCKY COUNTRY.

Q. O.K. then, why are so many adults cracking up?

A. BECAUSE THINGS ARE GREAT AND WE'RE THE GOOD GUYS.

Q. Why are the children cracking up? WHY?

A. Because we are free.

Leunig

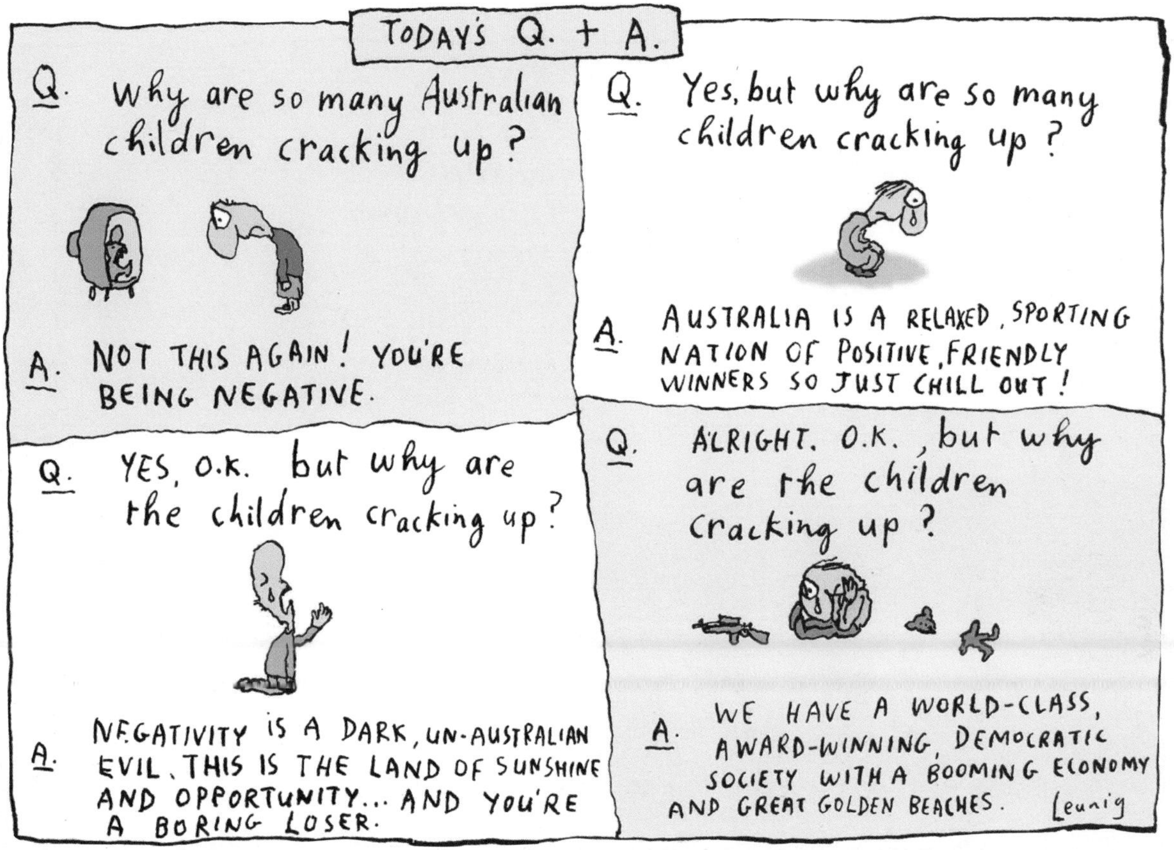

TODAY'S Q. + A.

Q. Why are so many Australian children cracking up?

A. NOT THIS AGAIN! YOU'RE BEING NEGATIVE.

Q. Yes, but why are so many children cracking up?

A. AUSTRALIA IS A RELAXED, SPORTING NATION OF POSITIVE, FRIENDLY WINNERS SO JUST CHILL OUT!

Q. YES, O.K. but why are the children cracking up?

A. NEGATIVITY IS A DARK, UN-AUSTRALIAN EVIL. THIS IS THE LAND OF SUNSHINE AND OPPORTUNITY... AND YOU'RE A BORING LOSER.

Q. ALRIGHT. O.K., but why are the children cracking up?

A. WE HAVE A WORLD-CLASS, AWARD-WINNING, DEMOCRATIC SOCIETY WITH A BOOMING ECONOMY AND GREAT GOLDEN BEACHES.

Leunig

THE TOWERS OF BABBLE

For every hill there is a tower.
For every dill there is the power
To send the message crisp and clear:
"You are there and I am here...
And ain't that just AMAZING!"
And where the heart was gently grazing
On the wild, sweet horizon,
There are metal towers to hurt your eyes on.

Leunig

HONEY, I CAN EXPLAIN, THOSE PHOTOCOPIES ... IT WAS ONE OF THOSE STUPID OFFICE CHRISTMAS PARTY THINGS ... SOMEBODY GOT A BIT HIGH SPIRITED AND SAT ON THE PHOTOCOPIER WITH NO KNICKERS ON AND A FEW COPIES WERE MADE OF THEIR BOTTOM ... IT'S JUST A CHRISTMAS JOKE.
YES ALAN BUT IT'S YOUR BOTTOM!
Leunig

The 3 A.M. WAKE-UP

Yet again
You wake at 3 A.M.
THE HOUR OF BLACK TRUTH.

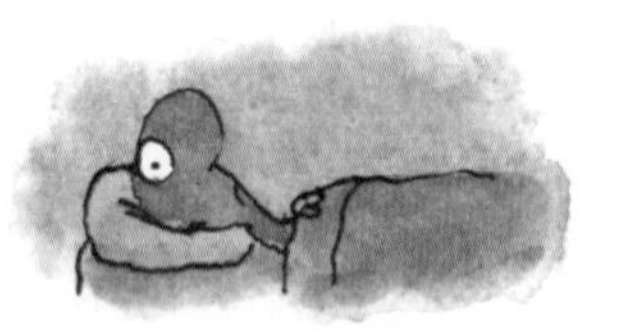

While you were sleeping
All meaning has collapsed.
Now only darkness exists.

Poor little plankton of the night,
You have been swallowed
By the great whale of DOOM.

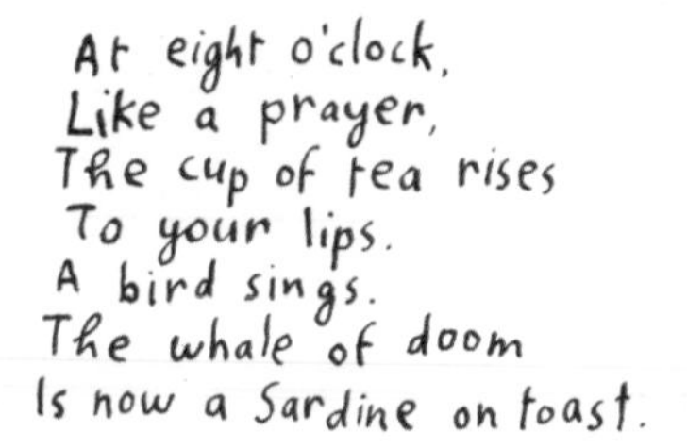

Down, down. Down you go
Into SHEER FUTILITY.
"It's all impossible" you groan.
Then you disintegrate
Into UNCONSCIOUSNESS.

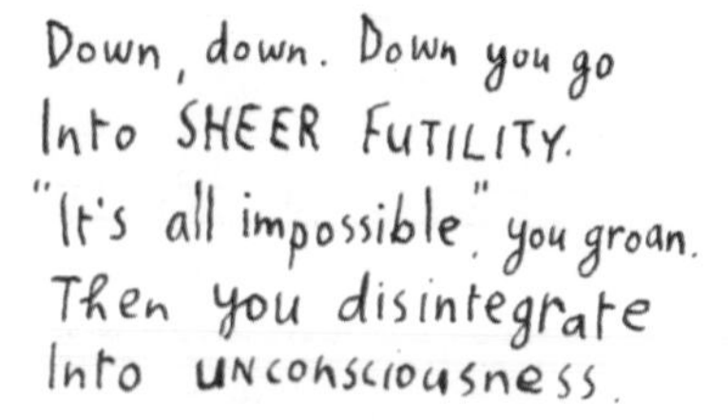

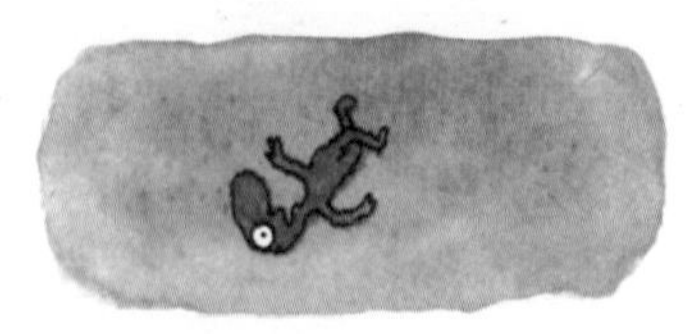

7.30 A.M.
Finds you at the table
Reconstructing your personality,
Rebuilding civilization.
THIS takes half an hour.

At eight o'clock,
Like a prayer,
The cup of tea rises
To your lips.
A bird sings.
The whale of doom
Is now a Sardine on toast.

Leunig

DOORSTOP INTERVIEW WITH GOD.

And what's that you're carrying?

Leunig

Father, what's the difference between a bad guy and a good guy?

A bad guy cuts your head off and a good guy blows your head off.

MESS
ACCOMPLISHED
Leunig

... me and Phil took an "Operation Iron Hammer" approach with family matters and I must say it's all been very interesting ...

Leunig

Mr CURLY'S New Year Resolutions

1. I shall think more about ducks.
2. I shall whistle more and do more of my bird calls.
3. I shall have more afternoon naps.
4. Urnm... that's about all I can think of at the moment.
5. Oh yes... I've just remembered; I will finish composing my mandolin concerto called "The Duck Concerto"
6. ... and maybe something about butterflies.

Leunig

Mr Curly's cure for summer melончholia (a condition caused by eating too much melon).
Leunig

IF YOU SEE ANYTHING MYSTERIOUS OR UNUSUAL, JUST ENJOY IT WHILE YOU CAN
Leunig

New Wine Releases ... (with quotes from labels)

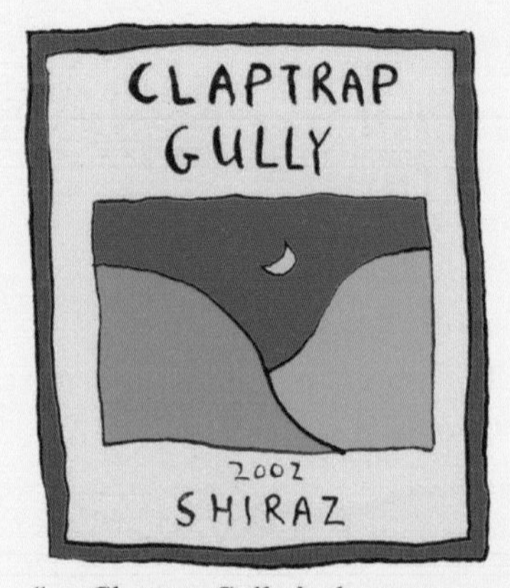

" ... Claptrap Gully is the name given to the bar in the pub where our advertising agency creative directors have lunch and dream up new wine labels... "

" ...It is said that many years ago our chief winemaker conducted an illicit, tempestuous affair with an actress named Beryl. To this day vineyard workers still unearth nail files, perfume bottles and cigarette lighters said to have fallen from Beryl's handbag during the wild, nocturnal love trysts amongst the Pinot Noir vines... "

" ...The creek which borders our Chardonnay paddock is locally famous for the abundance of condoms which can be seen floating on the current or washed up along the banks. We have named this sensuous, pleasure-driven wine in honour of the stream which irrigates our vines..."

Leunig

Here is a news flash ...
.. A live football player transport has overturned on the Eastern freeway....
Cages were damaged in the collision and a number of football players have escaped into the surrounding suburbs ...
Leunig

Harold darling...
what are the symptoms
of bird flu?
Leunig

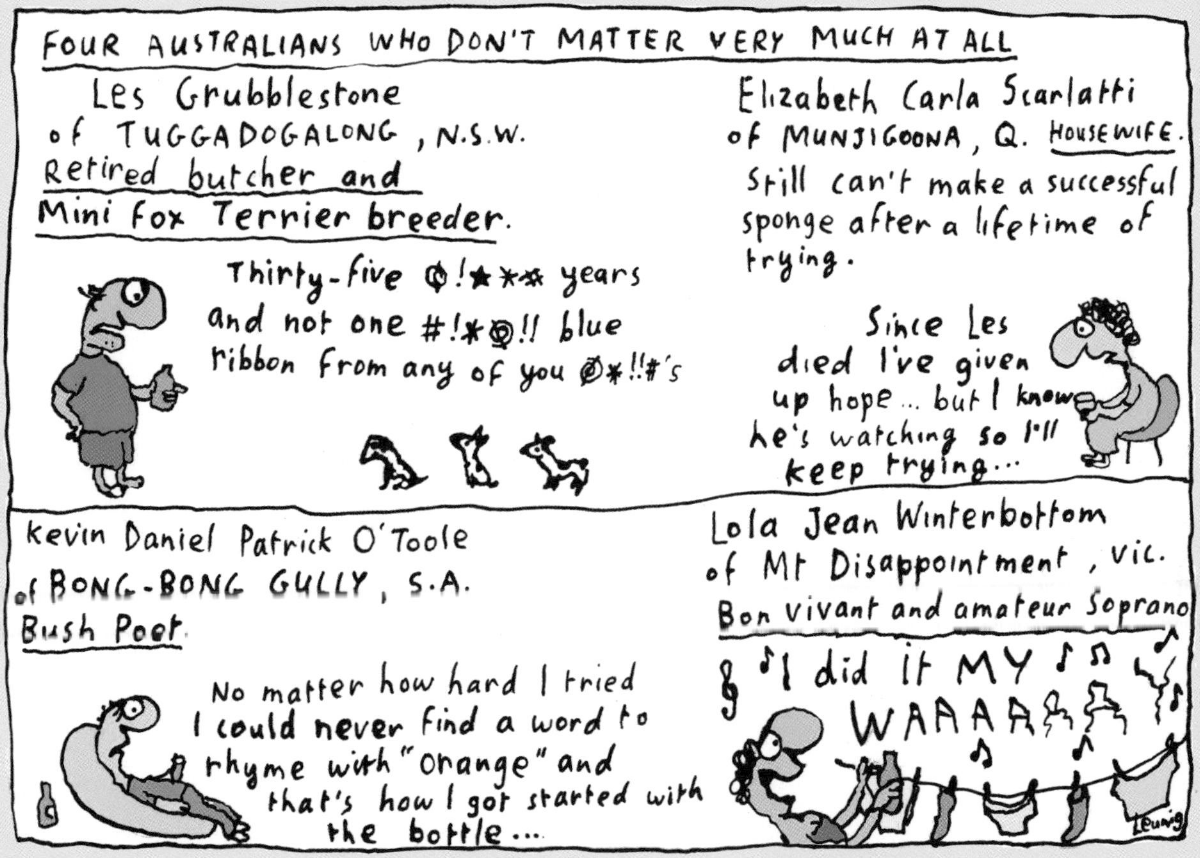

FOUR AUSTRALIANS WHO DON'T MATTER VERY MUCH AT ALL

Les Grubblestone
of TUGGADOGALONG, N.S.W.
Retired butcher and
Mini Fox Terrier breeder.

Thirty-five ¢!★** years
and not one #!*@!! blue
ribbon from any of you Ø*!!#'s

Elizabeth Carla Scarlatti
of MUNJIGOONA, Q. HOUSEWIFE.
Still can't make a successful
sponge after a lifetime of
trying.

Since Les
died I've given
up hope ... but I know
he's watching so I'll
keep trying ...

Kevin Daniel Patrick O'Toole
of BONG-BONG GULLY, S.A.
Bush Poet.

No matter how hard I tried
I could never find a word to
rhyme with "orange" and
that's how I got started with
the bottle ...

Lola Jean Winterbottom
of Mt Disappointment, vic.
Bon vivant and amateur Soprano

♪ I did it MY ♪♫
WAAAAAA

LEUNIG

We need a new defence force which is small, quick, clever and efficient.

Have we considered a large pack of fox terriers sir?

We *have* considered the fox terrier option...

and...?

...and splendid though they are in battle, obedient and disciplined — courageous in deportment and deed...

yes sir...

Alas, on ceremonial occasions, they cannot manage a slow march. Their feet move too quickly. An absolute fiasco. A total farce. A complete cock-up.

What a pity sir.

Leunig

Leunig

WE DIDN'T FLUSH THE KORAN DOWN THE TOILET.
WE FLUSHED THE BIBLE DOWN THE TOILET.
"DO UNTO OTHERS..."
"LOVE YOUR ENEMY..."
"THOU SHALT NOT KILL"
- STRAIGHT DOWN THE TOILET.
Leunig

THAT'S WHAT YOU CALL "AMERICAN KNOW-HOW"
leunig

you can fool some
of the people
all of the time...

... and you can fool
all of the people
some of the time.

But you only need
to fool a majority
of the people for one
day every few years...

... and you've got
a democracy!

Leunig

THINGS
ARE
GREAT
Leunig

MAKE SECURITY A PRIORITY!
As you know, miniature enemy frogmen have infiltrated our water pipes, sewers and drains in preparation for a major terror attack on Australia. These tiny, evil killers are already in the pipes of your home waiting for the signal to attack. It could be when you are in the shower, the pool or on the toilet! Don't take any chances. Invest now in the new
MINI-FROGMAN ELIMINATOR
The MFE detects and removes mini-frogmen in a simple, novel and hygenic action which combines conventional 4-stroke technology with the latest hydraulic laser principles. Protect your family and send for our free brochure today.
Leunig

ALWAYS LOOK ON THE BRIGHT SIDE
Leunig

Samantha drinks
BINGE LAGER.

Emma drinks
BINGE CREEK CHARDONNAY.

FIONA drinks
OLD BINGE whisky.

They drink together
at the BINGE BAR.
Season's greetings to
Samantha, Emma and
FIONA.

Leunig

Father's Day Gift Catalogue
MOBILE PHONE - SHAVER.
Now dad can shave and attend to those important calls as he drives to work.
TRIBAL DRUM WITH EMAIL FACILITY.
Now dad can access those vital business messages while he's connecting to the lost tribe of his soul and following his bliss
SAXOPHONE TELEVISION WITH CORDLESS ELECTRIC DRILL.
Now dad can watch current affairs, play the blues and attend to those odd jobs around the house.
WRAPAROUND SUNGLASSES WITH CONCEALED TEAR CATCHERS AND REAR DOWNPIPES.
Now dad can cry without anybody noticing.
Leunig

FREE !
ELVIS ALERT KIT
A MESSAGE FROM THE PRIME MINISTER OF AUSTRALIA
" My fellow Australians, I have provided you with this Elvis Alert kit, to protect you from Elvis Presley and the terrible threat he poses to our way of life. Elvis lives and we must be vigilant and not shirk our responsibilities or the tough decisions. If you see him, tell us. You will notice a fridge magnet has been included ."
THE PRIME MINISTER
HOW TO OPERATE THE FRIDGE MAGNET.
① Hold magnet between forefinger and thumb.
② Hold magnet 5MM from fridge door.
③ Release grip on magnet.
If you see Elvis, do not attempt to capture him. Ring the ELVIS ALERT hotline. (FREE CALL)
IF ELVIS APPROACHES YOU, DO NOT UNDER ANY CIRCUMSTANCES LOOK INTO HIS EYES.
FOR FURTHER INFORMATION ABOUT FRIDGE MAGNETS VISIT OUR WEBSITE: WWW.FRIDGEMAGNET.COM
HURRY LAST DAYS.
MONARO CV8
2001 Model, 5.7 Ltr Auto,
Leather Interior,
Like New.
$53,990
Leunig

"HOWARD" FIGHTING VEHICLE MK2 UNVEILED

The new improved "Howard" Fighting Vehicle Mk2 (pictured below right) was unveiled in Kapooka this week. This deadly power-pack (codenamed "The Beast") will be manned by the crack new Australian unit "Johnnie's Raiders" to spearhead a daring programme of pre-emptive strikes against Asian terror camps. Designed to deliver awesome, lethal force into the enemy backyard and catch him with his pants down, the Mk2 includes all the hi-tech features of the Mk1 (pictured below left), but will feature an improved central body hinge for enhanced zigzagging, plus some reworking of the duco on the bonnet panel. Inset photograph shows the Prime Minister at the controls. "This is our knockout punch in the war against terror," he said.

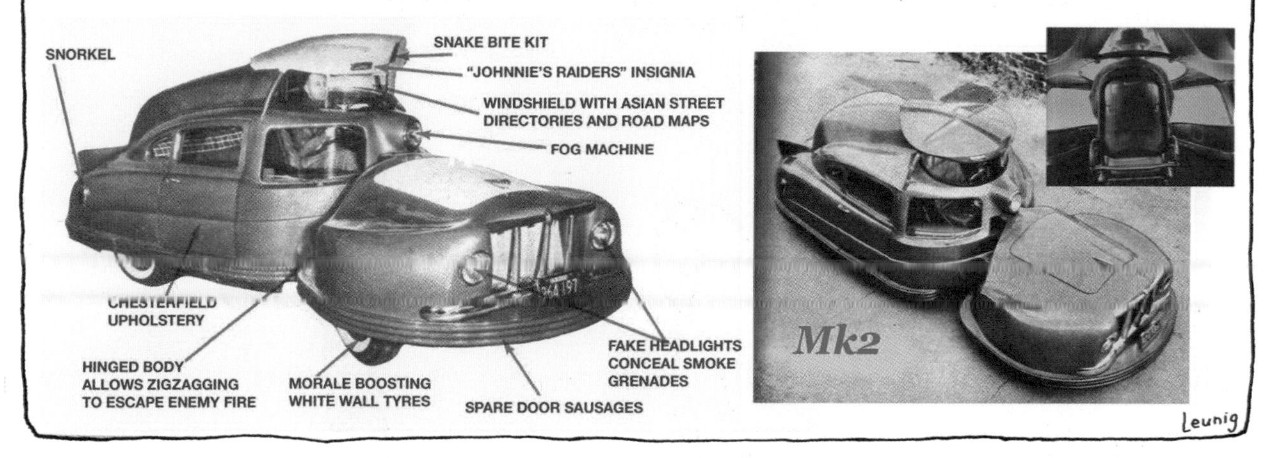

The Two Depressing Things

A most depressing thing occurs
But no one minds and no one stirs,
Which means you've ended up with two
Depressing things depressing you.

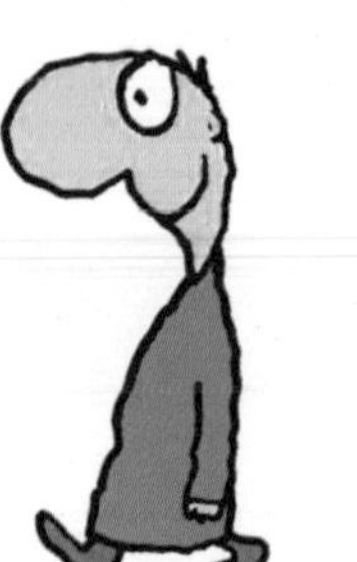

Leunig

OH JOYOUS PRAISE

Oh joyous praise
and love to thee
So innocent and
football free
To give thy sacred
Saturday
To flowers and fish
and birds at play
And wandering gently
in the sun
What need hast thou
to know who won
So innocent and football
free
Oh joyous praise
and love to thee.

Leunig

WELCOME TO
CURLY FLAT
A GOATED
COMMUNITY
Leunig

Exclusive INTERVIEW with MOUNT EVEREST

After years of cold silence the world's most famous mountain speaks to us at last.

What are you reading?
The clouds and stars. The writing on the wall.

What are you listening to?
The sound of heavy breathing. Mobile phones ringing. – Kurt Cobain.

What are you angry about?
The tall poppy syndrome.

What are you exultant about?
Just being me.

What's your idea of the perfect weekend?
To climb Sir Edmund Hillary and enjoy the view from the top of his head.

Who would you most like to sit next to on a plane?
Mount Vesuvius.

What song do you never want to hear again?
Climb every Mountain.

What's your greatest foible?
My north-east ridge.

What would you never give up?
My height above sea level.

What would you never do again?
Be so complacent.

If there were one word left to you in the English language, what would it be?
Avalanche.

Who do you find inspiring?
All volcanoes.

Who would you most like to meet?
Jacques Cousteau.

What is your ultimate holiday destination? Why?
New York for some peace and quiet and because it's there.

Leunig

Leunig

THE PASSION OF CHRIS
CHRIS... YOU'RE FANTASTIC. I CAN'T GET ENOUGH OF YOU... YOU BIG BEAUTIFUL MAN.
CHRIS! get out of bed this instant you lazy, useless worm. I've had a GUTFUL of you...
leunig

Various Bishops
GAY
STRAIGHT
STRAY
Leunig

NINE CHILDREN, WHO MAY HAVE BECOME TERRORISTS, KILLED BY AMERICAN WARPLANE IN AFGHANISTAN
... summertime ... and the livin' is easy ...
Leunig

That's quite an explosive suicide belt you've got there, Craig.
Leunig

TOTAL SECURITY!

Be safe. Catch the NUDE BUS. no hidden bombs.

.. of course, this doesn't mean that the terrorists have won...

Leunig

Hail to Prince Barry and Princess Cheryl of the Windy Flat Shopping Complex.
Some say they have no purpose; that they are anachronistic relics, that they do not earn their keep, that they are deeply flawed as individuals.
And this may well be so, but that's not the point. The point is that we all need a fairy-tale couple who are beyond our reach.
$2
...otherwise we are condemned to live with the drab ceaseless banality of the rich, the famous, the powerful and the glamorous always being shoved in our faces.
Leunig

One of the world's most beautiful things
Is the sight of a gentleman drying his wings
As he prepares for his flight to the sun;
Poor little innocent, dear little one.

Sad is the wondering look in his eye
Lingering there at the edge of the sky.
Why did it happen? How was it done?
Poor little innocent, dear little one.

Leunig

Ian Thorpe I am not.
Yet there's something I have got
Which gives a man a better chance:
Ian Thorpe underpants!

They're navy blue. They're fantastic!
With Ian's name on the elastic.
I hitch them up to indicate
That Thorpie is my closest mate.

If I fall beneath a bus,
At least I know there'll be a fuss;
In Casualty they'll sing and dance,
"Ian Thorpe underpants!"

Leunig

SEEDS and PETALS
No abortions, please!
It's compulsory to be born
Into this wicked world, oh little pawn.
The sanctity of life must be upheld;
The bombing of the town, the forest felled,
The poisoned river, the poisoning of hearts,
The smoking rubble, the body parts:
Parts of husband, daughter, son and wife
And the beautiful sanctity of life.
Leunig

Leunig

HOW TO CURE YOUR ADDICTION TO SELF HELP BOOKS
Leunig

... it's so amazing when we anti-climax together...
...we must be meant for each other.

The rich are getting richer.

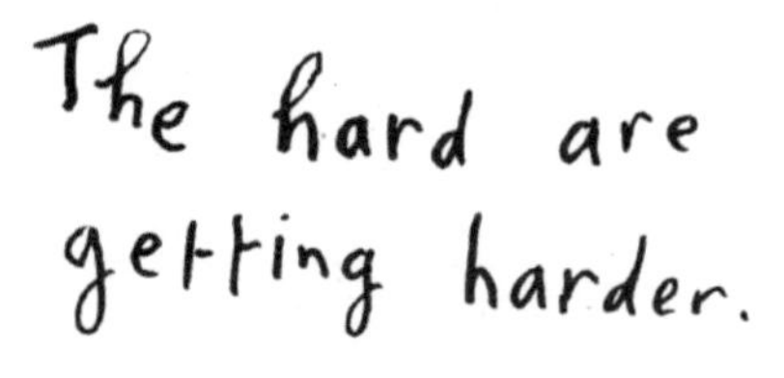

... and the frightened are getting frighteneder...

Leunig

the alliance is strong. It takes great dedication to suck and lick at the same time
Leunig

David Hicks...
you are charged
with being evil,
dangerous and
menacing ...

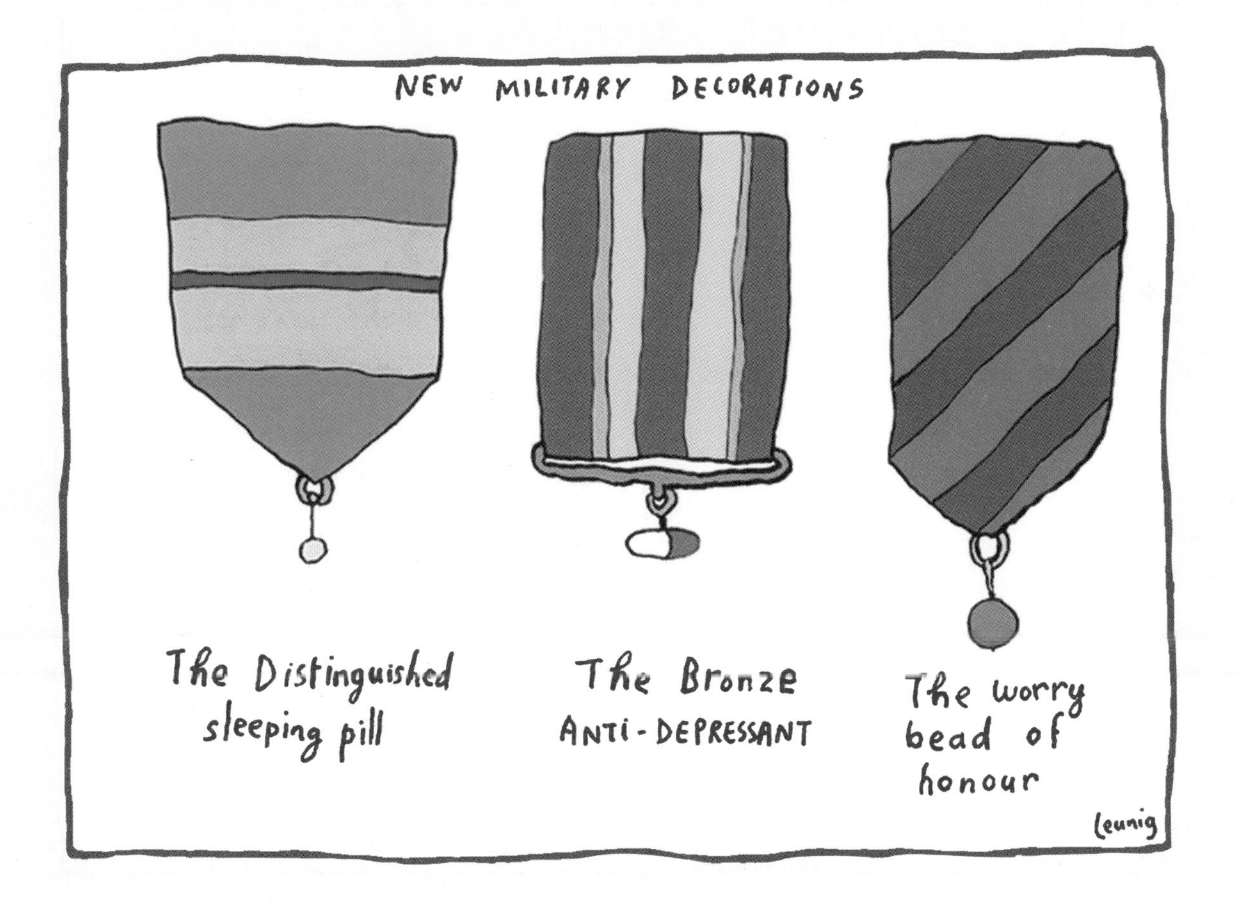
NEW MILITARY DECORATIONS
The Distinguished sleeping pill
The Bronze ANTI-DEPRESSANT
The worry bead of honour
leunig

STRANGE BUT TRUE
The INVASION of IRAQ was where...
... the most memorable war cries were produced by the MEDIA.
... and the most memorable photographs were produced by the SOLDIERS.
STRANGE BUT TRUE
Leunig

Leunig

"Look at that! Brilliant! You kill the leader and you nip the whole movement in the bud."

And you will find a lowly stable and a baby lying in a manger...

..and you will take control of the situation and impose security measures

...and you will sanitise and disinfect everything and get rid of the animals which are a health risk...

...and you will gather statistical data and connect the electricity and install central heating

...and you will introduce democracy and teach the parents to better themselves in a new global economy.

And you will show the child how to invest and be a winner with positive attitudes and good contacts and good ADVICE...

and if they Resist...

...if they resist, call this number ...report the situation...

...and wait until a team of experts arrive.

So long as lowly stables exist there can be no peace on earth...

Leunig

You are charged with attempting to think bad thoughts about Americans.

Data from a mind-reading satellite indicate that you have been thinking...

...that America is behaving like the Mafia...

and that America is behaving like the Nazis.

YES, BUT THEN I CONCLUDED THAT AMERICA WAS JUST BEHAVING LIKE AMERICA..

Leunig

SORRY
COACH

SOH
REEE,
SOH
REE
SOH-
REE.
SOH-
REE.
SOHH
OHH
-OHH-OHH
RREEEEE
SORRREEE

STANISLAVSKI METHOD.
CREATIVE VISUALIZATION.
IMAGINE THAT YOU
ARE SORRY
GO ON...
GO ON...
TRY...
SSSSSS...
SSSS...
SSSOFT...
S-S-SORE...
SSSAUSAGE
SSSS...
SS- SISSY
SUCKHOLE...
SS... SSSS...
COME ON...
THAT'S CLOSE.
NEARLY THERE.
COME ON.

The hunt for Osama Bin Laden is...
...ON FOR YOUNG AND OLD.
...WHAT SELLS NEWSPAPERS.
... BETTER THAN LOOKING AT YOURSELF IN THE MIRROR.
IT'S...
... ALL HIS FAULT.
...WHAT YOU'D EXPECT.
... A CIRCUS.
This time WE'LL GET...
...THE EVIL SWINE.
... TOLD MORE LIES.
.. OUR HANDS ON ALL SORTS OF STUFF.
AFTER WE GET HIM THE WORLD WILL BE...
... SAFER.
... DESTROYED BY A HUGE ASTEROID.
... OURS!
Leunig

Leunig

THE WAR AGAINST TERROR
2000 years ago
(MIDDLE EAST)
JOURNALISM, COMMENT, ANALYSIS
BAD GUY
BEST AND FINEST SPECIAL FORCES LIBERATOR
"HIGH-VALUE" PRISONER WITH SUSPECTED "LINKS"
JOURNALIST, COMMENTATOR, COLUMNIST
BLEEDING HEART
HAND WRINGER
WET LEFTIE
Leunig

HEY MUM! THE AMERICAN EVANGELISTS ARE AT THE FRONT DOOR.
Leunig

The river is full of @!*#

The media is full of @#*!

Politics is full of *!#@

And you're full of @*!*

Leunig

... The trouble was... that flagpoles across the nation were mysteriously wilting.

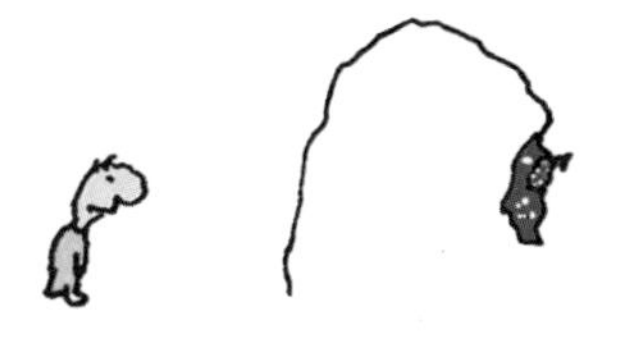

Experts were baffled but the poles were going all limp and shrivelled. AMAZING.

It was so embarrassing... so disturbing, but they wouldn't stay up any more. Flagpoles weren't what they used to be.

And furthermore, the children were becoming fat, miserable and nasty, while their parents got deeper into debt and deeper into anti-depressants... and the flagpoles wouldn't bloody well work. Bugger!

Colin Powell has had it tough
And now he says he's had enough;
He's going back to private life:
The house, the garden and the wife;
The golden memories returning
Of Baghdad and its children burning.
How nice to see a man retire
And put his feet up by the fire.

Leunig

Dear John, remember the night we sent the white powder to the Iraqis in
Baghdad? Here's the souvenir postcard. What a great night!
Your ol' mate George.
Leunig

Onward to Mars and the Moon

Honestly Basil, I don't mind your chardonnay drinking, your chattering, your latte sipping or your hand wringing... but why all at the same time?

Leunig

GOLCKET

AN AWFUL NEW GAME FROM THE AUSTRALIAN INSTITUTE OF SPORT
Leunig

There comes a moment when all the cables, leads, battery chargers and power adaptors we have ever owned gather together and assemble themselves around us and ask us the terrible question, "WHAT HAS HAPPENED TO YOUR LIFE?"
Leunig

The GOLDEN GOOSE JOURNALISM AWARDS, 2004
...and the next award for the evening is in a special new category.
It is the award for "The best piece of contrite or remonseful journalism".
This category recognises those in the media who warned us in no uncertain terms about Saddam's weapons of mass destruction...
...but who, upon discovering that they had been conned, went on to express sorrow for having promoted a ghastly war on the basis of such lies and deranged thinking.
Unfortunately there were no entries in this special section.... so we will move right on to the next award...
... which is also a new category: "The best piece of move-right-on journalism"...
Many entries were received and all of a VERY HIGH STANDARD.
... and the winner is...
leunig

Dogs Who Know When Their Masters Have Voted for War

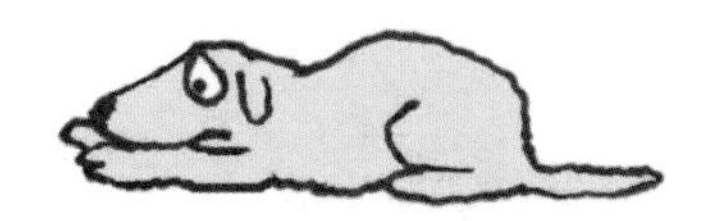

Leunig

... and if you paint
in a more realistic style
and do some nice, pleasing
landscape scenes, we might let you
join one of our proper artist societies.
Leunig

NO APOLOGY

This certificate of no apology, number CN 67439 S

is hereby issued to: Mamdouh Habib *by the*

Commonwealth Government of Australia

concerning the matter of false imprisonment

SIGNED John Howard

WITNESSED Philip Ruddock

DATE 12-1-05

Leunig

WHY THE LEFT WAS WRONG ABOUT CHRISTMAS by Steve Anvilbanger
The left is wrong about everything... particularly Christmas.
The people have voted with their feet.
They said it was about peace on earth and goodwill towards men!
Christmas is about getting hold of stuff, getting smashed and pigging out. Yeah!
But the real people know what it's about
STAR CLUB
It's about FREEDOM! Merry Christmas leftists! (YUK-YUK)
Leunig

SEA FEVER (inspired by John Masefield)

I must go down
to the sea again
To the lonely sea
and the sky
And all I ask
is a small shop
Where the dim-sims
fry.

Suddenly all the splendour and radiance was blocked out by something which had moved in front of it and now he stood in a murky gloom which poured down on him. "It will pass," he thought; but it didn't. It had no intention of passing. It enjoyed being in power too much and was rating surprisingly well in the opinion polls...

Leunig

Ah yes...
the economy
has never been
healthier
And the drugs
needed to
cope with it
have never been
more affordable..
Leunig

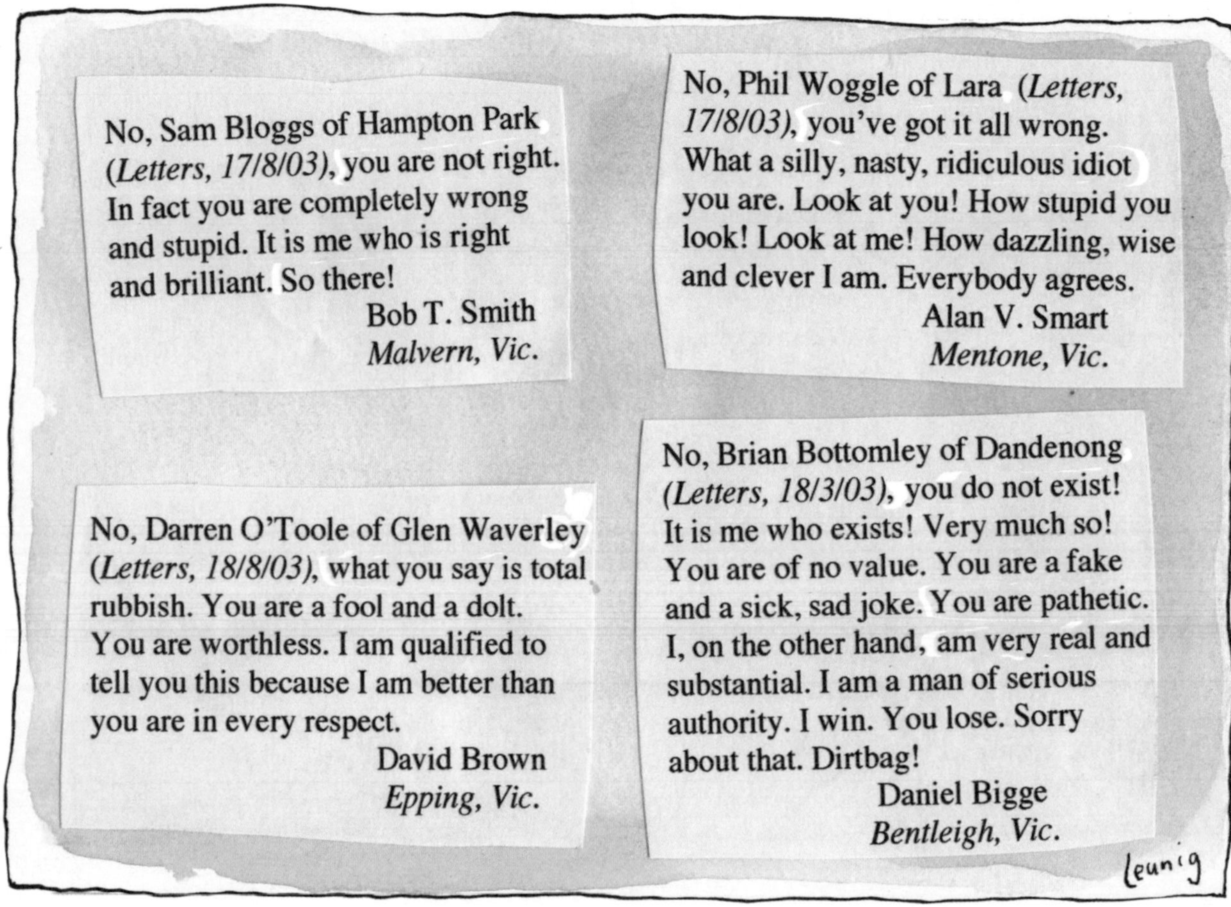

No, Sam Bloggs of Hampton Park (*Letters, 17/8/03)*, you are not right. In fact you are completely wrong and stupid. It is me who is right and brilliant. So there!

Bob T. Smith
Malvern, Vic.

No, Phil Woggle of Lara (*Letters, 17/8/03)*, you've got it all wrong. What a silly, nasty, ridiculous idiot you are. Look at you! How stupid you look! Look at me! How dazzling, wise and clever I am. Everybody agrees.

Alan V. Smart
Mentone, Vic.

No, Darren O'Toole of Glen Waverley (*Letters, 18/8/03)*, what you say is total rubbish. You are a fool and a dolt. You are worthless. I am qualified to tell you this because I am better than you are in every respect.

David Brown
Epping, Vic.

No, Brian Bottomley of Dandenong *(Letters, 18/3/03)*, you do not exist! It is me who exists! Very much so! You are of no value. You are a fake and a sick, sad joke. You are pathetic. I, on the other hand, am very real and substantial. I am a man of serious authority. I win. You lose. Sorry about that. Dirtbag!

Daniel Bigge
Bentleigh, Vic.

leunig

...I'm not sure whether I'm suffering from too much brutal reality or too many disgusting lies...
I'm suffering because too many disgusting lies is the new brutal reality.
Leunig

violence begets violence; it's as old as the hills...
... then we'll blow the hills to pieces!
Leunig

Father, what is "reliability"?

Reliability is the ability to tell a lie over and over again...

...to lie and re-lie and re-lie until the lie seems to sound like the truth... THAT'S RELIABILITY
Leunig

He found God.

God spoke to him. God said, "help me, I'm wounded."

God lay bleeding on the ground.

"You're not God," said the man, "God is ALL-POWERFUL."

"I am all-vulnerable," said God, "I am in pain. I am at your mercy."

These words were so unbearable to the man, so infuriating, that he finished God off right there and then.

THINGS WHICH CANNOT BE MENTIONED
ONE DAY
Leunig

An entire civilization buried under layer upon layer of lies, untruths and falsehoods!
People's last dramatic moments preserved forever by an almighty shower of weasel words.
A civilization suffocated and frozen in time; trapped beneath a huge deluge of spin.
Humans unable to flee; a civilization entombed; a whole culture tangled in twaddle... mummified in ridiculous poses of bewilderment!
leunig

Men are born free
but everywhere they are
in chains.

WHAT A PITY...

SECURITY

... THERE MUST BE
SOME WAY OF GETTING
THEM BORN IN CHAINS..

SECURITY
Leunig

advertisement
WINSTON PRIVATE COLLEGE
At Winston College we are educating the leaders of tomorrow.
We teach award-winning spiritual and moral values.
These cherished values are taught in such a way that they are no hindrance to the economic and career opportunities of our graduates in later life.
Winston students are brilliantly trained in all the state-of-the-art skills of morality and spirituality by our staff of experienced experts who impart the tricky ins and outs, the secret methods and the latest techniques of respectability and fine character.
ENROL YOUR CHILD NOW.
Leunig

The Australian College of Torture

NOW ACCEPTING ENROLMENTS FOR 2005

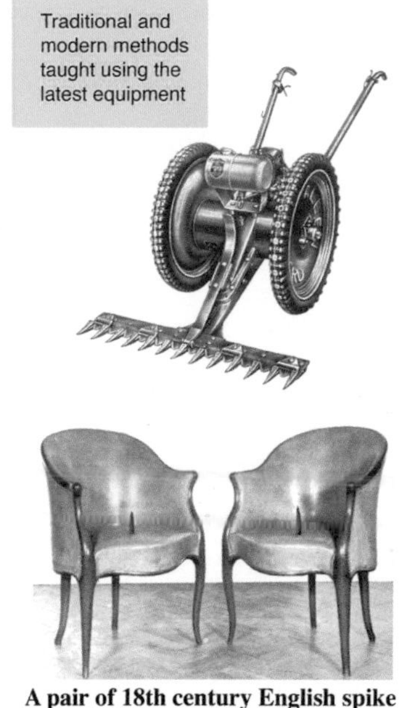

A pair of 18th century English spike chairs from our campus collection.

The Australian Torture College offers a two year diploma course (Dip. Tort.) which guarantees your place in the esteemed truth seeking professions. Follow your vocation and secure your future in this exciting growth industry by enrolling now.

ENDORSED BY THE AUSTRALIAN GOVERNMENT

"... normal, average Australians are practical people who understand what works and what gets the job done."

Leunig

GOOD FOR YOUR SOUL

Some push-ups with a dark cloud.

A few chin-ups on the MOON.

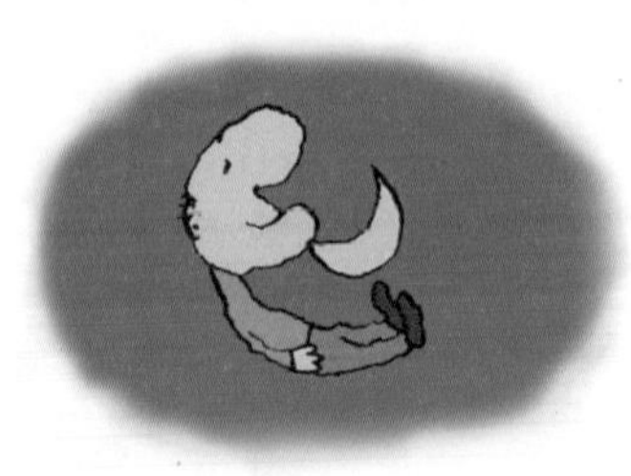

A few laps with the dog.

your lap with a couple of cats.

A quiet stroll around the mental block.

A chip off the old bloke.

SO ... IS THE GLASS HALF BROKEN
OR IS THE GLASS HALF FIXED ?

... the bride and groom will now accompany me to the vestibule to sign their performance contracts.

Some couples
are the salt of the earth
Some
are the salinity,
But the salt-and-pepper
shaker couples:
They achieve
DIVINITY.
Leunig